FOUR KEYS TO EFFECTIVELY SHARE YOUR FAITH

FOUR KEYS TO EFFECTIVELY SHARE YOUR FAITH
Greg Laurie

Revised Edition

A publication of

 harvest: greg laurie

Riverside, California
www.harvest.org

Greg Laurie is senior pastor of Harvest Christian Fellowship in Riverside, California.

Four Keys to Effectively Share Your Faith, Revised Edition

Text Copyright © 1992, 1993 by Harvest Ministries. All rights reserved. First Edition 1992. Revised Edition 2004.

Design: David Riley+Associates
Typesetting: Harvest Design
Copywriting: Harvest Publications
Copyediting: Harvest Publications

Printed in the United States of America.

ISBN 978-1-1932778-04-5

www.harvest.org

Contents

Key One: Personal Preparedness

One of the hardest things to do as Christians is to share our faith. Most of us get a good case of cold feet when the opportunity arises to tell someone about Jesus. We're often reluctant to share our faith for fear of having a person reject us and our message; yet God has given us clear marching orders to go into the world and preach the gospel, making disciples of all nations (see Mark 16:15; Matthew 28:19–20).

For some unknown reason, God has chosen to make known His unsearchable riches through us! Knowing how imperfect we are, you might ask, "Why doesn't He just use His angels to do the job?" No doubt He has chosen us because He loves us and wants us to enter into the most exciting adventure of the Christian life next to conversion itself: the opportunity to be used by God! As 2 Chronicles 16:9 says, "For the eyes of the Lord run to and fro throughout the whole earth, to show Himself strong on behalf of those whose heart is loyal to Him."

Witnessing is important for yet another reason. God has spiritually designated each of us with the need to both take in and give out. To fail to carry this out will result in spiritual stagnation! Proverbs gives us this pearl of truth: "The generous soul will be made rich, and he who waters will also be watered himself" (Proverbs 11:25).

Are you still uptight and nervous about sharing your faith? Relax. God has provided an antidote for cold feet, and He also has given us some sound principles that will enable us to lead others to Christ effectively. This antidote for our fear factor is a strong dose of boldness from the Holy Spirit. God will never ask us to accomplish anything He will not give us the power to perform. The calling of God is the enabling of God (see 2 Corinthians 3:4–6). If He has commanded us to go out and make disciples, we must be confident that He will be there to give us the ability to see the job through.

Along with the power of the Holy Spirit, however, we need to apply the principles of being "salt" and "light" so that we truly can be effective witnesses. In the Sermon on the Mount, Jesus provided some valuable insights on how we can do this (see Matthew 5:13–16). Let's take a moment to examine two of these important verses.

An Effective Witness Must Be Salt

When Jesus preached to the multitudes on the mount, He provided this illustration concerning effective witnessing: "You are the salt of the earth; but if the salt loses its flavor, how shall it be seasoned? It is then good for nothing but to be thrown out and trampled underfoot by men" (Matthew 5:13). Salt does two things. First, salt affects whatever it comes into contact with. If you put just a little salt in a glass of water, its taste is unmistakable. In the same way, one faithful Christian in an ungodly situation or place can make a difference. You will stand out by your words and actions.

Second, salt stimulates thirst. By living a godly life we can stimulate a spiritual thirst in the lives of others. Christians are to be "living epistles," written by God and read by people. One of the greatest compliments paid to a Christian by a nonbeliever is asking the question, "What is so different about you? Your life has a certain quality I admire, and I'd like to know more about it." Now that is being salt! Something as simple as taking your Bible to work and quietly reading it during your lunch hour can make an impact on a nonbeliever.

An Effective Witness Must Be Light

Similarly in His message to the multitudes, Jesus likened effective witnessing to light, saying, "Let your light so shine before men, that they may see your good works and glorify your Father in heaven" (Matthew 5:16). If salt is associated with living what we believe, then light signifies proclaiming what we believe. Too many believers try to be light without first being salt. They talk the Christian talk, but their lives fail to reflect a relationship with Christ. This discrepancy undermines their witness.

On the other side of the coin, many people are salt without being light. They live a godly life, but they don't tell people why! We must find a balance. As the Apostle Paul asked the Christians in Rome, "how can they call on him to save them unless they believe in him? And how can they believe in him if they have never heard about him?" (Romans 10:14 NLT).

So how can we be a "salty light," so to speak? Let me give you eight basic principles that I believe will help us as we strive to be effective lights and witnesses in the world.

[1] Effective sharing must be led by God's Spirit.

I believe that God wants us to be "sharp shooters," not "machine gunners." I've seen machine-gun evangelists who gauge their success by the number of people they can share Christ with in an hour. I question the effectiveness of this technique. It often appears that all they're looking for is another notch on their belts. We must learn to let the Holy Spirit lead us to the right person at the right time when sharing our faith. When a person comes to Christ, that decision will be a result of God's work, not ours.

Jesus said, "No one can come to Me unless it has been granted to him by My Father" (John 6:65). No brilliant argument is going to win over another person. If someone can be argued into the kingdom, they also can be argued out. Conversion must be the work of the Holy Spirit, and it must be in God's timing. That's why the Scripture tells us to be prepared to share the gospel message "in season and out of season" (2 Timothy 4:2). We never know when we will be called into action, and we don't want to miss out on opportunities from God simply because we're not paying attention.

[2] Effective sharing is grounded in a knowledge of God's Word.

The Lord has told us to preach the gospel, not morality, religion, personal opinion, or a particular church. The Apostle Paul writes in 2 Corinthians 4:5, "For we do not preach ourselves, but Christ Jesus the Lord . . . ."

Although our message may begin with a personal testimony or illustration, the thrust of it must be the Word of God! As a spiritual soldier, we must remember to take up the "sword of the spirit," which is God's Word (see Ephesians 6:17).

What if Philip had not known much about the Scriptures when he met up with the Ethiopian as the Bible describes (see Acts 8)? How would he have answered this man when asked, "Of whom does the prophet say this . . . ." (Acts 8:34)? Because Philip knew and understood God's Word, he not only was able to explain the passage of Scripture in question, but he also was able to lead the Ethiopian to Christ.

How do we get to know the Bible? One of the best ways is to commit Scripture to memory so that God can bring the right verses to mind when we need them. We must never neglect this powerful witnessing tool, for God promises, "My word . . . shall not return to Me void, but it shall accomplish what I please, and it shall prosper in the thing for which I sent it" (Isaiah 55:11).

[3] Effective sharing takes time.

It is far better to sit down for an hour with one person than to throw out trite clichés to fifty people in that same amount of time. Some of the most profound things Jesus ever said were found in His one-on-one conversations. He took time with these individuals (see John 3–4). We need to be willing to do the same, looking at the time we spend with someone as an investment in that person's life.

In some cases, a person will learn more about the Christian life by spending time with you during your daily routine than if you were to lead that individual in a two-hour discourse on Christianity. As Billy Graham once said, "Some things are caught, not taught." We must remember that we are not called to make converts, but disciples. As we allow our nonbelieving friends and coworkers to see our faith in action on a more personal level (i.e., inviting them over for dinner, taking a trip to the beach, going shopping, etc.), our words will often have more weight.

[4] Effective sharing is sincere.

For evangelism to be effective it must begin with a genuine concern for the lost; the Apostle Paul had such a concern. He so desired his own race to come to Christ that he said, "I have great sorrow and continual grief in my heart. For I could wish that I myself were accursed [or separated] from Christ for my brethren, my countrymen according to the flesh" (Romans 9:2–3). Paul was actually willing to suffer separation from God if he could be confident that his countrymen would come to know Jesus.

[5] Effective sharing is flexible.

In 1 Corinthians, Paul encourages us to tailor our approach, though not our message, to those we are trying to reach for Christ:

> And to the Jews I became as a Jew, that I might win Jews; to those who are under the law, as under the law, that I might win those who are under the law; to those who are without law, as without law…that I might win those who are without law, to the weak I became as weak, that I might win the weak. I have become all things to all men, that I might by all means save some. (9:20–22)

Paul refused to be constrained by cultural and racial barriers. He always remained flexible. When he spoke to Jews and God-fearing Greeks at the synagogue in Antioch (Acts 13), he was very up front and direct in his gospel presentation. Yet when Paul spoke to the Gentile philosophers and thinkers on Mars' Hill (see Acts 17), he was much more subtle, arousing their curiosity by referring to an altar on the premises that was dedicated to "an unknown god." Paul simply adjusted the bait for different kinds of fish. Evangelism is meeting someone at his or her level in order to bring that individual to Christ's level without compromising the truth of the gospel.

[6] Effective sharing is discerning.

When Jesus talked to Pontius Pilate, Pilate asked Him various questions. Jesus noticed that Pilate was showing some interest, so He responded to the man. But when Jesus was brought before Herod, He gave no answers. Why did Jesus relate so differently toward these two men? In Pilate, He saw a hunger, and He responded accordingly. In contrast, Jesus knew Herod only wanted to see a few "magic tricks." We also need to be discerning so that we will not "cast our pearls before swine," offering the truths of God to someone who is not genuinely interested. Some people are antagonistic and argumentative, and they really have no desire to hear the truth. Rather than anger someone who's uninterested, I think it's best simply to present the truth and move on.

Jesus continually exercised discernment as He talked to people. When He spoke with the woman at the well, He drew upon her interest in the water by asking her to give Him a drink (see John 4). As the story goes, the woman was amazed that Jesus, a Jew, asked her, a despised Samaritan, for a drink. Sensing her curiosity, Jesus then threw out some "bait," saying, "If you knew the gift of God, and who it is who says to you, 'Give me a drink,' you would have asked Him, and He would have given you living water" (John 4:10). This statement of the Lord aroused her interest, and she responded, "Sir, give me this water, that I may not thirst . . . ." (John 4:15). Jesus then had an open door to present the message of salvation.

So, next time you encounter a nonbeliever, remember that simple and personal questions, coupled with discernment, will often draw people out of their quiet shells and open many doors to sharing your faith.

[7] Effective sharing is tactful.

By definition, *tact* is "the intuitive knowledge of saying the right thing at the right time." A good example of tact is once again found in the story of Philip's encounter with the Ethiopian eunuch (see Acts 8). As Philip heard the Ethiopian reading from Isaiah, he simply asked, "Do you understand what you are reading?" (Acts 8:30).

A number of more judgmental Christians might have shouted, "Did you know you're going to burn in hell unless you repent?" Obviously such a statement would not have resulted in the Ethiopian's conversion. I've often heard nonbelievers attack Christians for their lack of tact. Some of those criticized believers go away feeling persecuted. They should realize, however, that they're not being persecuted for righteousness' sake; they're being persecuted for being obnoxious! A fruitful witness is a tactful witness.

[8] Effective sharing is backed by love.

This final principle is the most important one we need to employ. Whenever Jesus came into contact with people, He genuinely loved them. He took a sincere interest in each individual. Such love and concern will speak volumes before we even utter a word.

It seems that there are very few people who really care anymore—everybody wants something. The world today is flooded with religious cults, which are Satan's way of flooding the market with imitations. As it is now, most nonbelievers are suspicious of anyone with something to say about God. That should not stop us, however. In fact, those imitations and suspicions ought to motivate us even more to make the truth known. Why? Because we have been given the same love in our hearts that Jesus had when He walked on this earth. Our edge over these spiritual counterfeits is that love combined with the Word of God will not return void. The cults do not have Jesus' real love for people, but we do! We are told that God's love has been poured out in our hearts by the Holy Spirit (see Romans 5:5).

Some Things to Think About . . .

- When was the last time you told someone about Jesus?
- When was the last time you shared His love with someone in need?

Why not ask God for His boldness right now? Ask the Holy Spirit to lead you to someone who needs Christ. Then spend time with that person, showing a genuine concern for his or her well-being. If that individual is not "your type," be willing to adapt. Learn of his or her interests and exercise discernment as to how and when you might tactfully approach that person with the gospel. Love that individual with the love of God, and then share the truth of the gospel. Then you'll see how "the goodness of God leads you to repentance" (Romans 2:4). I guarantee that the blessing will be yours.

Key Two: the Power of Prayer

This may come as a surprise to you, but the truth is that sharing your faith is like being in a battle. The only difference is it's a spiritual battle for the souls of people. There are people whose souls rest on the very message of the gospel. And the weapons that we fight with are not the weapons of the world. On the contrary, the weapons we fight with possess divine power to demolish the strongholds we face. This is why every Christian must utilize the spiritual weapons God has given to us.

One of the greatest spiritual weapons we possess is prayer. This powerful weapon is a classic example of why the early church turned their world upside down. The first-century believers constantly encountered difficult situations and rallied to defeat the enemy with the secret weapon of prayer. An old hymn said it best when it proclaimed, "Satan trembles when he sees the weakest saint upon his knees." The book of Daniel gives us a good example of the role of prayer in the spiritual battle that faces us today. Daniel was praying and twenty-one days later, an angel came with the answer to his prayer—along with an amazing story. The angel went on to explain that God heard Daniel's prayer and dispatched him from heaven—along with an answer. But he was overcome by a more powerful demon. So God sent Michael the archangel to free the angel from the demon's stronghold. Twenty-one days later, there he was with the answer to Daniel's prayer.

Interesting, isn't it? It's a reminder that God's delays are not necessarily His denials. It just may be that as you are praying for a certain person to come to Christ, a behind-the-scenes spiritual battle is taking place. That's why you need to keep praying. We need to be persistent in our prayers for the lost, whether it appears that God is answering them or not.

The New Testament reminds us of a similar story involving James and Peter, the apostles of Christ. King Herod Agrippa had begun to persecute the church, and the Apostle James (the brother of John) would be his first martyr. So Herod had James beheaded. The Bible then tells us that the execution of James pleased the religious leaders of the time. When Herod realized this, he had Peter arrested as well. Now things were looking really bleak for the church. James was dead. And it was only a matter of time until Peter faced the sword of Herod as well.

In these drastic and hopeless times, what details does the Bible provide about the church's reaction? Do we read that the church immediately organized a boycott of all products made in Rome? No. Do we read that they decided to have Herod overthrown and initiated a write-in campaign? No. The church reacted in a manner we don't see enough of these days. They prayed. In fact, the Bible says, "the church prayed very earnestly for him [Peter]" (Acts 12:5 NLT). Though all other doors were closed, one remained open. It was the door of prayer. This was and is the church's secret weapon. It was the door into the presence of God.

The way through to Peter was the one through to God. While the church prayed, there was Peter, chained in a dark prison guarded by two soldiers and even more at the prison gates. It looked as if it was only a matter of time until Peter was dead. But the Lord answered the prayers of the church. The Scripture says, "Suddenly there was a bright light in the cell, and an angel of the Lord stood before Peter" (Acts 12:7 NLT). Like in the book of Daniel, God sent an angel. The prayers of the church prevailed.

Unfortunately, Christians today typically turn to prayer as a last resort. When people get headaches, what is the first thing they do? They take a Tylenol. Then the headache persists and they call the doctor. But it rarely crosses their minds to pray and say, "Lord, would You just heal me right now." But in the case of Peter's impending death, prayer crossed the minds of the early church.

I think we all could learn a few principles from the church's prayer for Peter. Let's consider those principles and what made them so powerful.

[1] The prayer that has power is the one that is offered to God.

Immediately, you might think, Greg, isn't all prayer offered to God? Not necessarily. Often in prayer our mind is taken up with what we want rather than with our heavenly Father. We can flippantly throw out a request and never even think of the One we are speaking to. We must remember, He is not our butler who art in heaven. He is our Father who art in heaven. We would be wise to contemplate the One we are speaking to. This is God Almighty. He is the Creator of the heavens and the earth. He is the perfect and flawless holy God. If we think about that for a moment, if we let it sink in, I suggest it will change the way we pray.

In a similar manner, before we share our faith, we need to offer a prayer to our Father who is in heaven. We need to offer to the Lord the person we want to share our faith with. We need to pray, "Lord, you have told me in Your Word You are not willing that any should perish, but that all should come to repentance; therefore, I pray that this person opens his eyes to You. Help him to see his need for You, Lord. Help him to put his faith in You. I bring him before You." Praying for the lost is something every Christian must take part in consistently and persistently. This brings us to the second principle found in the prayer of the early church.

[2] The prayer that has power is prayed with intensity.

Look at what verse five says, "Peter was therefore kept

in prison, but constant prayer was offered to God for him by the church." Too often we pray flippantly. We may pray, "Lord, I pray for so in so. Save him. Amen." Or it might even be "Lord, save the whole world. Amen." Then we ask ourselves, I wonder why my prayers are never answered? Maybe it's because those types of prayers are not prayers of intensity.

This phrase "constant prayer" could be translated "they prayed earnestly." Another way to translate it is "they prayed stretched out." Have you ever dropped something only to have it fall just beyond your reach? That is how the church prayed. They were grasping and reaching out for the throne of God. This type of prayer speaks of a soul in a stretch of earnest desire—praying with intensity. In other words, a powerful prayer is a prayer into which we put our whole soul—stretching out toward God with a passionate and agonizing desire. A lack of heart is one of the main reasons our prayers possess little power.

When is the last time you prayed with intensity for someone? You may say, "I prayed for them once and they didn't get saved, so I just gave up." Really? You need to keep praying. As Jesus said, "Ask, and it will be given to you; seek, and you will find; knock, and it will be opened to you" (Matthew 7:7). That phrase could be translated, "keep asking, keep seeking, and keep knocking. Don't give up." In your prayer life, you need to keep asking. You need not to give up. You need to pray and pray and pray again for that unsaved person.

[3] The prayer that has power is offered to God by the church.

The book of Acts doesn't say that one person prayed for Peter. No, it says that "constant prayer was offered to God for him by the church" (Acts 12:5). Underline that last phrase, "by the church." There is power in united prayer. Jesus said, "I say to you that if two of you agree on earth concerning anything that they ask, it will be done for them by My Father in heaven" (Matthew 18:19).

That is a powerful promise. And one that I think has been misinterpreted by some people who have a different agenda. They say if you just agree together, if you have faith, if you believe it, then you can speak it into existence. Just get together and pray believing. Does that mean if three of us get together and pray for a gold plated Rolls Royce, we'll receive it? No. The idea here is not just of three people agreeing together. It is the idea of three people agreeing together for something that is the will of God. The point here is that you are praying with other believers, understanding what God wants and praying in accordance with that, but recognizing that there is power in united prayer.

That is why you need to meet with other believers and pray for people you know who are not saved. You need to call up your friend and say, "Will you pray with me for the people I want to share the gospel with?" Not only that, but together you keep bringing those people before the throne of God—day in and day out. It doesn't always have to be a long prayer. You and your prayer partner can pray for them when you have lunch. You can pray for them on your drive to work. (Keep your eyes open of course.) You can pray for them all of the time—bringing them before the throne of God.

[4] The prayer that has power is prayed doubtingly.

This principle is not as commendable as the first three, but it comes out clearly in this story about Peter. When Peter arrived at the home of Mary, the mother of John Mark, no one believed it was him (see Acts 12:14–15). Yes, they prayed fervently. Yes, they prayed together. But they also prayed with doubt. I am not saying we should pray with doubt. What I am saying is even when we don't have all the faith one could hope for, God will more than meet us half way. Again, there are those who say you must have complete and total faith. They will claim that if you lack any faith while you pray, then it is your lack of faith that is causing that prayer not to be answered. No doubt there is a place for faith in prayer— a very important place. But I suggest that we are to come with as much faith as we have and leave the rest in the hands of God.

I cite as an example the story of the man with the demon possessed boy. He came to Jesus and said, "Lord, have mercy on my son" (Matthew 17:15). Jesus said in response, "If you can believe, all things are possible to him who believes" (Mark 9:23). Immediately the father of the child cried out with tears running down his cheeks, "Lord, I believe; help my unbelief" (Mark 9:24). What did Jesus say to this? Did He say, "Sorry, buddy. You don't have enough faith. Get out of here." Of course He didn't say that. Jesus healed that child. That father came with as much faith as he could muster, and Jesus met him more than half way.

The early church acted in the very same manner, they prayed to God with what little faith they had. There they were praying. "Lord, we pray for Peter. You allowed James to be killed—but please spare Peter. Send Peter to us." Then suddenly someone knocked at the door. So a servant girl named Rhonda went to open the door and recognized Peter's voice. But instead of opening the door, she ran and told the others. How did the rest of the believers react to Rhonda's news about Peter? They told her, "You are beside yourself!" (Acts 12:15). But then they decided to check it out for themselves. So they opened the door and they were astonished. It was Peter. Despite their doubt, God honored their prayer. He more than met them half way.

[5] The prayer that has power changes things.

Look at how life changed as a result of prayer. The chapter opens with James dead, Peter in prison, and Herod triumphing over the church. But the chapter closes with Herod dead, Peter free, and the Word of God triumphing. That is how prayer works. That is why we need to pray.

Some of us may feel God hasn't called us to preach. But He has called us to pray. Whether you're new at sharing your faith or you're a seasoned evangelist, prayer is essential to reaching the lost for Christ. I challenge you,

I urge you, and I beg you to pray for the unsaved people in your life. We know what this is about. We know the gospel is the only hope for the world. We know that the solution to our problems is spiritual. Our battle is not "against flesh and blood, but against principalities, against powers, against the rulers of the darkness of this age, against spiritual hosts of wickedness in the heavenly places" (Ephesians 6:12). Therefore, let us—as the church—commit ourselves to praying with intensity for the lost.

Key Three: Answering the Objections

Most of us know what it is like to share the gospel with someone who insists on barraging us with a mass of arguments and questions that are very difficult to answer. Such an experience usually leads us in one of two directions: either we determine never to confront a person with the gospel again (which would be a disgrace), or we seek to find the answers and follow the advice of Scripture. In his epistle, the Apostle Peter gives a good piece of biblical advice concerning sharing the message of Christ:

> Always be prepared to give an answer to everyone who asks you to give the reason for the hope that you have. But do this with gentleness and respect, keeping a clear conscience, so that those who speak maliciously against your good behavior in Christ may be ashamed of their slander. (1 Peter 3:15–16 NIV)

The word *answer* comes from the Greek word *apologia*, which means "to present a verbal defense to everyone who asks you for a logical explanation." People should not throw out logic, intelligence, or common sense when they become believers. In fact, Scripture tells us that part of God's transforming work in our lives is "the renewing of our minds" (Romans 12:2).

Nevertheless, we are reminded throughout the New Testament that we are not to rely on our reasoning abilities alone. When Paul stood before his accusers, he gave brilliant verbal defenses for his faith, yet he did not rely on arguments alone. Concerning this matter, Paul said,

> For Christ (the Messiah) sent me out not to baptize but [to evangelize by] preaching the glad tidings (the Gospel), and that not with verbal eloquence, lest the cross of Christ should be deprived of force and emptied of its power and rendered vain . . . For the story and message of the cross is sheer absurdity and folly to those who are perishing and on their way to perdition, but to us who are being saved it is the . . . power of God. (1 Corinthians 1:17–18 AMPLIFIED)

For that reason, we must do our best to be prepared to give a verbal defense to anyone who asks, while recognizing that our message must remain simple and point back to Christ!

The following questions and excuses represent just a few obstacles you may encounter as you talk with nonbelievers. I've given some brief answers, but you might gain even greater insight by looking at some of the books suggested in the appendix: "Continuing to Dig Deeper."

[1] How do I know the Bible is true?

"I can't believe the Bible—it's so full of contradictions!" I'm sure you've heard this line at one time or another. But try to get someone who uses that argument to name even one inconsistency. For many, you'll find this question is just a "smoke screen."

Such people may say to you, "You quote the Bible to prove the Bible. That's circular reasoning." But is it? After all, the Bible was written over a period of about fifteen hundred years by more than forty authors from a wide variety of backgrounds and locations. The Bible includes the writings of Joshua, a military general; Daniel, a prime minister; and Peter, a fisherman. The authors of Scripture come from such diverse places as the wilderness (Moses), prison (Paul), and a remote island called Patmos (John). The Bible also was written on three different continents: Africa, Asia, and Europe. Moreover, its text was written in three different languages: Hebrew, Aramaic, and Greek.

As remarkable as those facts are, the most amazing thing about the Bible is its unity and consistent flow of thought. When 2 Timothy 3:16 says, "All Scripture is given by inspiration of God," it does not mean that God turned these writers into "keys of a typewriter," simply punching out the letters or dictating the words to them. Instead, God worked through the different personalities of people like Jeremiah and Paul, much like an artist uses different brushes on a canvas for the complete portrait. The message is the same, yet it is distinctively colored by each author's God-given, unique character and personality.

Another interesting fact about the Bible is that it accurately predicts the future. So far the prophecies of the Bible have been filled with one hundred percent accuracy. How can this be true? You must realize that, for God, telling the future is as easy as telling the past. It's history in advance!

For example, Scripture predicted Jesus' birthplace, type of ministry, mode of death, and Resurrection with pinpoint accuracy. The odds of Jesus fulfilling even eight of those recorded prophecies is the same as if the state of Texas were covered with two feet of silver dollars, with all but one minted in the same year, and that one different dollar being picked out of the whole lot by someone who was blindfolded. Yet Jesus fulfilled no less than thirty-eight Old Testament prophecies during His time on earth! No other writing can make that claim.

[2] If God is so good, why does He allow evil in the world?

This question always appears at the top of people's lists of questions about God! Why does He allow babies to be born blind? Why does He allow wars to be waged and injustice to exist? Why does He allow tragedy and suffering?

The general tendency is to blame God for evil and suffering and pass all responsibility on to Him. In the classic statement of the problem, either God is all powerful but not all good, and therefore doesn't stop evil, or He is all good but not all powerful, and therefore can't stop evil.

In actuality, both statements are inaccurate and the blame misplaced: humankind, by its own decision, brought evil into the world. We must remember that God did not create humanity to be evil, but perfect—unaging, innocent, and eternal. God also gave humankind the ability to choose between right and wrong, and Adam and Eve made their choice in the Garden of Eden. From that point, sin entered the world. Had humanity never sinned, the curse of sin would not have come as a result. The Apostle Paul substantiated this in his letter to the Romans, "When Adam sinned, sin entered the entire human race. Adam's sin brought death, so death spread to everyone, for everyone sinned" (Romans 5:12 NLT).

When faced with this question, the point we must keep in mind is that people—not God—are responsible for sin. "But why didn't God make people so we couldn't sin?" someone might ask. God did not make us robots or wind-up dolls, because He made us in His image with the ability to choose.

Wars, for instance, are not initiated by God, but by people! James 4:1-2 appropriately states, "Where do wars and fights come from among you? Do they not come from your desires for pleasure that war in your members? You lust and do not have. You murder and covet and cannot obtain." The truth of the matter is that the evil in this world does not come from God; it comes from our sinful living.

The Scripture also tells us that we will reap what we sow (see Galatians 6:7). A good example of this is the problem of starvation in India, once one of the

most fertile lands in the entire world. Because of the
prevalence of Hinduism in the region, however, many
inhabitants of India believe that animals are sacred,
representing a reincarnated life-form. Consequently,
since cows are considered sacred, the people refuse to
kill them, starving as a result. Rats, too, are given sacred
status, so the people allow these rodents to eat the food
supplies and spread disease. The people are reaping
what they have sown. The rampant spread of AIDS is
also an example of the sowing and reaping process. If
people would only abstain from premarital, extramarital,
homosexual, and bisexual relationships, the risk of
getting the disease would be virtually nonexistent.

Of course, God can remove suffering and pain. He still
answers prayer and heals people, performing miracles
today. Yet even if God allows people to go through a
certain difficult circumstance, Christians have the hope
that one day "God will wipe away every tear from their
eyes; there shall be no more death, nor sorrow, nor
crying. There shall be no more pain, for the former
things have passed away" (Revelation 21:4).

[3] How can a God of love send people to hell?

If someone throws out this question, remind them that
God doesn't send anyone to hell. We send ourselves.
God did not create hell for humankind, but for the devil
and his angels. People who have chosen to reject God
and His plan of salvation will one day hear the words
recorded in Matthew 25:41, "Depart from Me, you
cursed, into the everlasting fire prepared for the devil

and his angels." God doesn't want anyone to go to hell. The Bible is replete with verses that back up God's compassion and longsuffering toward humankind (see Ezekiel 33:11; John 3:16; 2 Peter 3:9). This logically leads us to the conclusion of the author of Hebrews, when he states, "How shall we escape if we neglect so great a salvation?" (2:3).

[4] What about those who have never heard?

It's important to keep in mind that when we don't understand something, we must fall back on what we do understand. As I mentioned earlier, God is not willing that any should perish. He clearly loves us. Acts 17:31 says, "He has appointed a day on which He will judge the world in righteousness…." Though we don't know how He will deal with these people spiritually, we do know that He is more than fair. (For more insight into this topic, study Romans 2:12–16. You will find that no one will be condemned for not hearing about Christ).

Nevertheless, each of us will be accountable for what we have heard. The person with whom you are talking is now personally responsible for what he or she knows (not what the Pygmy in Africa knows). That individual can no longer plead ignorance!

[5] There are too many hypocrites in the church!

No doubt this is true, but it is equally true that there are many godly people who really do live out the Christian life. More often than not, people will bring up this excuse if you've effectively "rolled away the stone" of questions they've fired at you. When this complaint surfaces, remind them that their eyes should be fixed on Christ, not on people, because people, even if they are saved, will sin. Jesus is our only perfect model, "the author and finisher of our faith" (Hebrews 12:2).

[6] Why is Jesus the only way?

The world offers many ways a person can search for God, but it is important to note that there is only one way that leads to life! There's only one way that leads to the Father. That way is Jesus Christ.

After sin entered the world through Adam, God instituted animal sacrifice as a means of reconciling our relationship with Him. As Hebrews 9:22 says, "Without shedding of blood there is no remission [of sin]." Because "all have sinned and fall short of the glory of God" (Romans 3:23), God sent Jesus, who became the final sacrifice. For that reason, to suggest that Jesus is one of many ways to God and eternal life, is to make a mockery of His death and to call Him a liar!

Jesus repeatedly declared throughout the Scriptures that He was the only way to God. While speaking with the Pharisees, Jesus told them, "All who ever came before Me are thieves and robbers, but the sheep did not hear them. I am the door. If anyone enters by Me, he will be saved, and will go in and out and find pasture" (John 10:8–9). Jesus made a conclusive statement to the Pharisees that He was the only way—He is the door to heaven! In the last twelve hours of His ministry, Jesus had been speaking with His disciples and declared, "I am the way, the truth, and the life. No one comes to the Father except through Me" (John 14:6). There was no other way. If humankind could have reached God any other way, then Jesus would not have had to die.

Key Four: Presenting the Plan

I came to know Jesus after hearing a message from a youth leader who was holding a Bible study on my high school campus. I'll never forget the words he quoted from Jesus, saying, "You're either for me or against me." I looked at the small group of committed Christians, who formed that little study group, and then I looked at myself. I knew they were for Him—they were for Jesus—and I also knew that I wasn't. But deep in my heart, I desperately wanted to be. When the speaker summoned those forward who wanted to become Christians, I waited and I waited. It was certain social suicide to join up with these "Jesus freaks." But those words kept echoing in my head. "You're either for me or against me." And so I finally came. I wanted to know this Jesus they spoke of!

Through the power of prayer and God's Word, you will share your faith with some one much like me. The Holy Spirit will work in that person's heart, and he or she will want to know the Jesus you spoke of. When that opportunity arises, I want you to be prepared to lead that individual into a saving relationship with Jesus Christ.

That's why I want to share with you seven points I often use when I preach the gospel. They were adapted from a Billy Graham message at Madison Square Garden in the fifties. Just like I adapted them from Billy, I pray that you too will put them into your own words, so that you will be sharing from your heart, and not from the pages of a book. Below are those seven points in what I like to call "God's Plan of Salvation."

[1] We Are All Sinners

The first thing we need to establish with people is that they are sinners. People do not like that title. The one word that defines all sin is the Greek word *hamartia*, which means "to miss the mark." What is God's mark? Jesus said, "Be perfect, just as your Father in heaven is perfect" (Matthew 5:48). Unless a person is perfect, he or she has missed the mark; therefore, that individual is a sinner.

The Bible is clear. We all are sinners and need the salvation of Jesus Christ. The Prophet Isaiah spoke about this when he said, "All we like sheep have gone astray; we have turned, every one, to his own way; and the Lord has laid on Him the iniquity of us all" (Isaiah 53:6). The Apostle Paul echoed these words in his letter to the Romans, saying, "All have sinned and fall short of the glory of God" (Romans 3:23). And lastly, as the author of 1 John writes, "If we say that we have no sin, we deceive ourselves, and the truth is not in us" (1 John 1:8). There is no way around it. Every person is a sinner and is in need of Jesus Christ.

[2] The Result: Death!

Next, we need to establish what the result of sin is. Paul made this point clear, saying, "The wages of sin is death . . . ." (Romans 6:23). Every one of us has missed God's mark. Every one of us falls short of being perfect. The result of that failure is death. We are only getting what we deserve and we are bringing judgment upon ourselves. One thing we all need to remember is that God never sends anyone to hell. We send ourselves there by rejecting His truth.

[3] The Resolution: Christ's Death on the Cross

At this point, we can let them know the solution: Christ died for our sins. Below are three Scriptures you can share to express God's solution for our sins:

1. "For God so loved the world that He gave His only begotten Son, that whoever believes in Him should not perish but have everlasting life. For God did not send His Son into the world to condemn the world, but that the world through Him might be saved." (John 3:16–17)

2. "He was wounded for our transgressions, He was bruised for our iniquities . . . ." (Isaiah 53:5)

3. "God demonstrates His own love toward us, in that while we were yet sinners, Christ died for us." (Romans 5:8)

Since we can never measure up to God's standards on our own, He has reached out to humanity. We cannot solve the problem of sin, but God, who is perfect, can and has. He has made available a way to reconcile us to Him.

[4] The Choice: to Accept or Reject Jesus Christ As Savior

If a person will acknowledge that he or she is a sinner and accepts the promise that Christ is the solution, then that person is at a crossroads. Either that individual must reject God's solution and accept the consequences, or he or she must accept Jesus Christ as Savior. What must a person do to accept this gift? Simply receive it! Jesus made this clear when He proclaimed, "Come to Me, all you who labor and are heavy laden, and I will give you rest. Take My yoke upon you and learn of Me. . . . for My yoke is easy and My burden is light" (Matthew 11:28–30).

[5] The Response: to Receive the Gift of Eternal Life

Jesus' invitation is clear. We must come to Him. All that remains is a response. The Apostle Paul said that God's gift "is eternal life in Christ Jesus our Lord" (Romans 6: 23). What do we have to do to receive that gift? Take it! In essence, Jesus stands at the door of our hearts and knocks, seeking entrance into our lives (see Revelation 3:20). What do we have to do to have Him come in? As Jesus said, just open the door, "Behold, I stand at the door and knock. If anyone hears My voice and opens the door, I will come in to him and dine with him, and he with Me" (Revelation 3:20).

In the first chapter of his Gospel, the Apostle John writes, "But as many as received Him, to them He gave the right to become the children of God" (John 1:12). We must receive Christ. How? By asking Him into our lives. If we have shared these truths with a nonbeliever, and that person wants to receive Christ, then we need only ask him or her to confess Christ as Lord. In fact, we need to pray with that individual at that very moment if he or she is willing to pray! There is no greater joy than to lead someone in prayer to receive Christ.

[6] The Assurance of Salvation

Following this, it is important that the new believer has some assurance that Christ has come into his or her life. Below are three ideal Scriptures you can share with a person who needs the assurance of salvation:

1. "This is the testimony: that God has given us eternal life, and this life is in His Son. He who has the Son has life; he who does not have the Son of God does not have life. These things I have written to you who believe in the name of the Son of God, that you may know that you have eternal life, and that you may continue to believe in the name of the Son of God." (1 John 5:11–13)

2. "Therefore, if anyone is in Christ, he is a new creation; old things have passed away; behold all things have become new." (2 Corinthians 5:17)

3. "As far as the east is from the west, so far has He removed our transgressions from us." (Psalm 103:12)

At this point, you may encourage the new believer to make a public confession of his or her newfound faith in Jesus Christ. To encourage them to confess their newfound faith, share Jesus' words from Matthew 10:32–33,

> If anyone acknowledges me publicly here on earth, I will openly acknowledge that person before my Father in heaven. But if anyone denies me here on earth, I will deny that person before my Father in heaven. (NLT)

[7] Making Disciples of Jesus Christ

Your part in sharing your faith is not over once someone makes a confession of faith in Jesus Christ. In fact, Christ has commanded every one of His followers to be disciple makers. Remember what Christ said before He ascended into heaven? Let's read about it in Matthew 28:18–20:

> And Jesus came and spoke to them, saying, "All authority has been given to Me in heaven and on earth. Go therefore and make disciples of all the nations, baptizing them in the name of the Father and of the Son and of the Holy Spirit, teaching them to observe all things that I have commanded you; and lo, I am with you always, even to the end of the age." Amen.

There are two very important things to consider in this statement of our Lord. First, in the original language it is a command. That is why we refer to this statement of the Lord as the Great Commission and not the "great suggestion." It was not a suggestion of Jesus that we make disciples of all the nations. It was and is a command. Secondly, these words were not merely directed to the original Twelve. They were given to all followers of the Lord. Christ has commanded every single one of His believers to be disciple makers.

What does it mean to make disciples? Jesus defined it in verse 20, "*teaching* them to *observe* all things that I have commanded you" (emphasis mine). To make disciples of all the nations means to teach people to observe what Jesus has commanded. This concept of making disciples of all the nations is the willing action of trying to win people to the Lord and then get them up on their feet spiritually.

Passing on the teachings of the Christian faith to a new believer is the responsibility of every Christian. Christ has called us to carry out this calling, this command. Make sure you make a passionate attempt to encourage the people you lead to Christ to live out the four following aspects of the Christian faith:

1. Read the Bible consistently and faithfully.
2. Spend time each day in prayer.
3. Fellowship and serve in a local Bible teaching church.
4. Share your faith in Christ with others.

The Apostle Paul substantiated Jesus' command to make disciples when he wrote, "So everywhere we go, we tell everyone about Christ. We warn them and teach them with all the wisdom God has given us, for we want to present them to God, perfect in their relationship to Christ" (Colossians 1:28 NLT). This is what we need to do. We must help people come to faith and then help them grow in their faith spiritually. This is our mission from God.

Appendix: Continuing to Dig Deeper

To be effective witnesses, we need to constantly study God's Word and learn more about ways to improve our presentation of Christ to others. The Apostle Paul was so well respected in the way he explained the gospel message that many Jewish leaders came to listen to him toward the end of his ministry. One instance of this is recorded in Acts 28:23–24, where it says,

> Many came to him [Paul] at his lodging, to whom he explained and solemnly testified of the kingdom of God, persuading them concerning Jesus from both the Law of Moses and the Prophets, from morning till evening. And some were persuaded by the things which were spoken, and some disbelieved.

It's important to remember that no matter how eloquent or inspiring your sharing of the gospel may be, some people still will not believe. Nevertheless, many others will. Keep in mind that the Holy Spirit will be the One ultimately to move a person to repentance. You will simply be the instrument God uses for accomplishing the task.

To better equip you for the challenges you will undoubtedly face in sharing your faith, here are some suggestions for further study:

- *The Impact Manual: Equipping Believers to Impact Their World*

- *Making God Known*

- *Handling Difficult Questions*

- *New Believer's Guide to How to Share Your Faith: First Steps for New Christians.*

- *The One-Minute Message*

Finally, nothing can substitute being fully grounded in the Scriptures themselves. Here are four final reading suggestions for preparing yourself to share the gospel with others:

1. Read John 4:1–26. Take note of how Jesus struck up a conversation wit the Samaritan woman and established rapport with her before He shared the truth of the gospel message with her.

2. Read the book of Acts. Study the different ways in which the believers of the early church shared their faith.

3. Read 1 Thessalonians 1:1–10. Here you will see the importance of your life being a living example as you witness.

4. Read 1 Peter 3:13–4:19. These passages will encourage you when you find opposition from others who are hostile to you and the gospel.

Dear Friend,

If you prayed to receive Jesus Christ as Lord and Savior while reading this book, then you have now begun a lifelong, personal relationship with Him. Your decision to follow Christ means God has forgiven you and that you will spend eternity in heaven with Him. The Bible tells us, "If we confess our sins, He is faithful and just to forgive us our sins and to cleanse us from all unrighteousness" (1 John 1:9).

To put your faith in action, be sure to spend time with God by reading the Bible, praying, going to church, and telling others about Christ. To help you in living out your faith, Harvest Ministries has a number of spiritual resources available to assist you in your relationship with God. You may write to us here at Harvest to receive spiritual resources. You also can receive resources when you register your decision to follow Christ at Harvest Ministries' Web site at www.harvest.org/knowgod. While you're at our Web site, be sure to visit the "Tools for Spiritual Growth" page. There you'll discover biblical teachings and resources that will encourage you as you learn to know God and share His love with others.

May God bless you as you grow closer to Him.

Sharing God's love,

Greg Laurie

PS: You can e-mail me personally at Greg@harvest.org.

Greg Laurie
HARVEST MINISTRIES

P.O. Box 4000
Riverside, CA 92514-4000

PastorGreg@harvest.org
www.harvest.org

PASTOR GREG'S DAILY DEVOTIONS

Get Connected Today!

Sign up today for Greg Laurie's daily e-mail devotions. You'll receive daily encouragement and relevant teaching in a quick, bite-sized format during the week, plus a longer, in-depth article on the weekends.

To get Pastor Greg's daily devotions, visit harvest.org.

HARVEST TOOLS

Helping you know God and make Him known

Visit harvest-tools.org to see Harvest Ministries' entire line of booklets, books, music, tracts, Bibles, and studies–available at discount prices for churches and ministries.

To order resources from Harvest Ministries, contact us at:

Harvest Resources
6115 Arlington Avenue
Riverside, CA 92504
Phone: 951.354.1392
FAX: 951.351.8045
harvest-tools.org

Notes

Notes